Gluten-Free Party Food

ALL THE FLAVOR, WITHOUT THE GLUTEN!

Happy Cooking!

BY: LINDSAY GARZA

Copyright © 2015 by Lindsay Garza

Photography copyright © 2015 by Lindsay Garza

Selected recipes first appeared on veggiebalance.com

All rights reserved. No part of this publication may be reproduced or distributed in any form or by any means, electronic or mechanical, or stored in a database or retrieval system, without prior written permission from the publisher.

ISBN 978-1516910120

This book is for entertainment purposes. The publisher and author of this cookbook are not responsible in any manner whatsoever for any adverse effects arising directly or indirectly as a result of the information provided in this book.

Printed in the USA

Jacket Design by Kevin Simon Design
Recipe Symbols by Sarah Snyder

Stuffed Jalapeño Poppers– See recipe on Page 22

All the flavor, without the gluten

ACKNOWLEDGEMENTS

To my invisible Internet friends, the readers of my blog, the eyes on my little corner of the Internet called Veggie Balance: You are my community and my muse; your love and sweet words mean more than you know. You make every endless hour working on posts, editing photos, and cooking failures worth it. You inspire me to continue to grow and have given me something that I love to do. Thank you, I love you all!

To Roland, aka "R" and the love of my life: Thank you for putting up with the concoction of meals and snacks I've made over the years and listening to my rambling on about photography and food when you have no idea what I'm talking about. Your support is unreal and more than I could possibly ask for. You're amazing and my life wouldn't be complete without you.

To Daddy Matty: Without your love and support pushing me on, I would not be writing this and never would have started Veggie Balance. Thank you for showing me it is possible to do what you love and not to be afraid of the unknown. Thank you for always being there and taking those phone calls when I needed another brain to bounce ideas off.

To my Mother: You might not realize it, but I believe you are the reason I have such a tenacious and strong-willed personality. Growing up, you proved to us that you can get through anything God hands you and be victorious. Thank you for being the most amazing, supportive mother during my years of sickness and always answering the phone when I needed someone to cry to.

CONTENTS

5	Acknowledgments
10	What You Will Find
13	Introduction
17	Favorite Staple Ingredients
19	Symbols Ledger

LET'S HAVE A PARTY!

22	Jalapeño Poppers
24	Loaded Potato Nachos
26	Cheesy Chili Cheese Dip
28	Buffalo Chicken Meatballs
30	Ham & Cheese Sliders
32	Deviled Eggs
34	Best Way to Boil Eggs
36	Pulled Pork Nachos
38	Bacon Wrapped Potatoes

BAR MUNCHIES

42 Baked French Fries

44 Fried Pickles

46 Onion Rings

48 Potato Wedges

50 Pico De Gallo

52 Barbecue Back Ribs

54 Chicken Fingers

56 Cheesy Garlic Bread

58 Blue Cheese Sliders

DIPPING, DUNKING, SCOOP WORTHY DIPS

62 Beer Ale Cheese

64 Best Guacamole Ever

66 Spinach Artichoke Dip

68 Queso Dip

70 Hummus Dip

DOLLOP WORTHY CONDIMENTS

74 Healthy Ketchup

76 Buffalo Dipping Sauce

78 Barbecue Sauce

80 Homemade Mayonnaise

82 Metric Conversions

83 About The Author

84 Index

WHAT YOU WILL FIND

<u>What are you going to find in the Gluten-Free Party Food cookbook?</u>
You will find healthy, all-natural recipes for gluten-free and non gluten-free eaters, all easily adapted for vegan, vegetarian, and dairy-free diets. With these recipes, entertaining a crowd has never been easier.

Simple to make, delicious to eat.

You will also find that my fingers make an appearance in almost every picture. Party food should not require utensils! *(Yes, that's the reason my fingers are in most of the shots.)*

Not only will you find no need for utensils, but every recipe is tailored to a 100% gluten-free diet and all-natural ingredients. There are also recipes that fall into the grain-free, vegetarian, vegan, paleo, and dairy-free dietary requirements with some modifications. When available, these adaptations are at the bottom of the recipe.

<u>On page 19, you will find a handy symbols ledger of special dietary needs.</u> These symbols are included at the top of each recipe for a quick overview: Gluten-Free, Dairy-Free, Low Calorie, Paleo, Vegetarian, and Vegan friendly.

You will find that each recipe is simple, to the point, healthy and less than 400 calories per serving. **Each recipe also includes the nutrition information for calories, fat, carbohydrates, sugar, protein, sodium, and fiber.**

In this book you'll get a little glimpse into my life, including my fur-family Cooper (pictured on right), produce in and from my garden, as well as staple ingredients from my kitchen. Simple, natural ingredients are a necessity in my home, perfect for transitioning into a natural, healthier, gluten-free lifestyle.

INTRODUCTION

Let me tell you the short story about myself. I was never a baker or cook, and I never ventured out past the steady taco dinner. I'd cook some ground beef, throw it in a shell, and bada bing bada boom, that was dinner my friends. My addiction to Mexican cuisine still runs deep, and I still make it for dinner at least once a week. Nonetheless, a home cooked dinner was a rare occasion. My food more often than not consisted of ordering it over the phone and picking it up from the restaurant.

After many years of battling gastrointestinal upset, fatigue, and infections that would run rampant in my body, I was sick of being sick. I never tied it to my food, nor did my doctors. That would be too simple, right?

After a massive sepsis infection, I was left with another crippling symptom: severe body aches and fatigue. That was the final straw. With no help or relief from the doctors, I decided to stop taking the prescribed medication, radically change my diet, and start taking care of myself. I eliminated processed foods, chemicals, and preservatives from my diet and introduced an all-natural approach to my meals, including antibiotic-free local meats and dairy. I eat plenty of organic and fresh produce as well, straight from my garden when in season. Along with my all-natural approach, I am also totally gluten-free. After two years of perfecting my diet, I have finally found what works for me.

How Did I Handle This Change?

Let me first say there were many small diet changes that rolled into a big fat diet success. I quickly found out that eating out is not the best choice for those with food allergies and intolerances. Conceding that I was no longer going to be able to eat my favorite comfort and finger foods from restaurants, I had to get creative and make them in my own kitchen. *GASP*

At first, since I rarely cooked at all, this seemed impossible. However, I decided my health and taking better care of myself were more important than convenience, so there I went, into the kitchen to begin this daunting task.

Turns out it wasn't as daunting as I thought and it even became a creative outlet for me. I found myself not following recipes and just winging it. It was the most liberating experience mixed in with a few total recipe failures. I started VeggieBalance.com to share my recipes and experiences in going gluten-free and taking my life back. At the same time, I discovered a passion for food photography. I became even more addicted to healthy food and the overall experience as my body began thanking me for finally taking care of it.

Within a couple of months, my symptoms began to dissipate and I finally felt like I had gained my life and my youth back from these crippling diseases. After about five years of battling my doctors, I was eventually diagnosed with fibromyalgia along with a gluten intolerance. My response? No medicine for me, just taking care of my body with natural food and exercise.

Symptoms I thought were normal like chronic heartburn, stomach pains, gastrointestinal upset, and skin rashes all went away when I eliminated gluten from my diet, and I've never gone back since. Just because I couldn't eat my favorite comfort foods in the restaurants didn't mean I could never eat them again, right? Not if I have anything to say about it.

I am a finger-food, ketchup-dipping fries kind of gal; always have been and always will be. Over the years I've re-created my favorite party and bar munchies to fit with my gluten-free diet. These recipes are my go-to when I crave a big plate of onion rings or fried pickles. Shoot, why can't I have both? With this book, you can!

What is My Take on Food?

My take on food is to keep it as simple and basic as possible. Massive ingredients and ten pages of instructions are the plague to me. Keep it simple my friends, for both my sanity and yours. There are a few ingredients that you might have to buy if you are new to the gluten-free lifestyle, but all the ingredients are simple, natural, fresh, and clean—the way nature intended us to eat.

When keeping it simple and natural, it is extremely important to consume antibiotic-free, grass-fed dairy and meat. These are what I use in any of my recipes that contain meat or dairy ingredients.

I do not believe that one specific diet works for everyone. We are all different and our bodies are different as well. If your body thrives on a vegan or vegetarian diet, that is awesome, but it does not mean that lifestyle is for everyone. **I find eating real food is what is most important.** Vegetables, nuts, clean meats, and fruits (in that order) are what my body thrives on. I don't care if you are Paleo, Vegan, Gluten-Free, or Vegetarian, the most important factor of all is eating real food the way nature intended.

So come dive into some finger-licking recipes with me!

"The food you eat can be either the safest and most powerful form of medicine or the slowest form of poison."
– Ann Wigmore

FAVORITE STAPLE INGREDIENTS

Potato Starch: This ingredient is fairly common in my recipes. It is just the starch extracted from potatoes. This simple ingredient is generally found in the health and wellness section and is useful for breading or used as a thickening agent in soups and sauces.

Potatoes: Potatoes are such an amazing food and a staple in my diet. They are a great source of vitamin B6, potassium, and a variety of phytonutrients that have antioxidant qualities.

Sour Cream: Though a great source of calcium and riboflavin, I personally love sour cream for its fats. I do not shy away from fat and intentionally eat extra fat that is naturally found in natural foods. It is important to opt for antibiotic-free and grass-fed dairy products.

Onions: Such a simple ingredient, but an amazing and versatile one. Onions have phytochemicals that improve the processing of vitamin C in the body and are a rich source of chromium, which helps regulate blood sugar.

Spinach: These dark leafy greens are another daily staple ingredient. Spinach has been shown to lower glucose levels and is high in potassium and fiber. There is more potassium in one cup of cooked spinach than one cup of banana. It also is high in vitamin A, a necessary vitamin for healthy skin and hair. Best of all, spinach is rich in iron which helps with metabolizing proteins and the production of hemoglobin and red blood cells.

Chicken Fingers – See recipe on Page 54

"You don't have to cook fancy or complicated masterpieces – just good food from fresh ingredients."
– Julia Child

SYMBOLS

 Gluten-Free

 Dairy-Free

 Paleo

 Low Calorie
Under 200 Calories

 Vegetarian

 Vegan

Cheesy Chili Cheese Dip– See recipe on Page 26

LET'S HAVE A PARTY!

Recipes for entertaining

JALAPEÑO POPPERS

Yields: 24 poppers

INGREDIENTS

12 jalapeños

12 slices bacon

8 ounces cream cheese, softened

1 ½ teaspoons garlic powder

1 teaspoon paprika

INSTRUCTIONS

Preheat oven to 400° F.

Slice jalapeños down the middle lengthwise, creating 24 pieces. Clean out the seeds with a spoon.

Slice each piece of bacon down the middle lengthwise, creating 24 pieces of bacon.

Place the softened cream cheese in a medium sized bowl. Fold in the garlic powder and paprika until fully incorporated into the cheese.

Begin preparing poppers by spooning cream cheese mixture into center of each jalapeño. Take one piece of bacon and wrap around jalapeño.

Continue until all are wrapped and place side by side in 9x13 pan.

Bake for 30-35 minutes.

Serve immediately.

NUTRITION PROFILE

Calories per popper	Total Fat	Total Carb	Sugars	Protein	Sodium	Dietary Fiber
51	4 g	1 g	1 g	2 g	118 mg	0 g

JALAPEÑO POPPERS

LOADED POTATO NACHOS

Serves: 5-6

INGREDIENTS

4-5 red skin potatoes, thinly sliced

2 Tablespoons butter

4-5 slices bacon, cooked, crumbled

3 ounces cheddar cheese, shredded

2 Tablespoons sour cream

¼ cup green onion, diced

INSTRUCTIONS

Preheat oven to 350° F.

Prepare a baking sheet by lining it with parchment paper.

Arrange thinly sliced potatoes on the baking sheet as you would for nachos, layering them just slightly.

Melt the butter in the microwave for 5-10 seconds.

Lightly brush the potato rounds with butter. Top with bacon and cheese.

Bake for 30 – 35 minutes.

Garnish with sour cream and diced green onion.

 Omit Bacon

NUTRITION PROFILE

Calories per serving	Total Fat	Total Carb	Sugars	Protein	Sodium	Dietary Fiber
207	11 g	20 g	2 g	8 g	196 mg	3 g

LOADED POTATO NACHOS

CHEESY CHILI CHEESE DIP

Serves: 12

INGREDIENTS

1 pound ground chicken or beef
2 Tablespoons taco seasoning
¼ teaspoon cayenne pepper
1 ½ cups black beans
1 cup salsa

2 Tablespoons butter
2 ½ Tablespoons potato starch
¼ cup half & half
1 cup shredded cheddar cheese
Fresh green onion, chopped

INSTRUCTIONS

In a large skillet, brown ground chicken or beef. Drain off excess oil. Mix in taco seasoning, cayenne, black beans, and salsa.

In a small saucepan, melt butter over medium heat. Add potato starch and stir in to form a paste. Slowly whisk in half & half.

Stir in cheese. It will turn into a thick paste.

Add the cheese paste into the chili skillet. Stir until well combined.

Sprinkle green onion on top and serve immediately or can keep warm in a slow cooker.

 Omit all ingredients after salsa.

TACO SEASONING: Per 1 pound of meat

2 tbsp. chili powder
1 ½ tsp cumin powder
1 tsp garlic powder
1 tsp onion powder
¼ tsp red pepper flakes
¼ tsp cayenne pepper
¼ tsp salt

NUTRITION PROFILE

Calories per ¼ cup	Total Fat	Total Carb	Sugars	Protein	Sodium	Dietary Fiber
170	10 g	9 g	0 g	12 g	184 mg	2 g

CHEESY CHILI CHEESE DIP

BUFFALO CHICKEN MEATBALLS

Serves: 5-6

INGREDIENTS

1 pound ground chicken
1 egg
3 Tablespoons potato starch
2 scallions, chopped
½ teaspoon garlic powder
½ teaspoon onion powder

BUFFALO SAUCE:

1 cup Frank's Red Hot® sauce
½ cup white vinegar
1 ½ Tablespoons paprika

INSTRUCTIONS

Mix together ground chicken, egg, potato starch, scallions, garlic powder, and onion powder. Fold ingredients together until well combined. Place in the refrigerator 15-20 minutes for easier handling.

Preheat oven to 400° F. Line two baking sheets with parchment paper.

Create inch size meatballs and place on the parchment covered baking sheets (approximately 24 meatballs).

Place in oven and bake 5-6 minutes.

While meatballs are baking, prepare the buffalo sauce, combining hot sauce, white vinegar, and paprika.

Remove meatballs from oven, place them in the crockpot, and cover with the buffalo sauce.

Set crockpot on low for 4 hours or high for 2 hours. For best flavor, cook on low as long as possible.

NUTRITION PROFILE

Calories per serving	Total Fat	Total Carb	Sugars	Protein	Sodium	Dietary Fiber
38	2 g	1 g	0 g	4 g	418 mg	0 g

BUFFALO CHICKEN MEATBALLS

HAM & CHEESE SLIDERS

Yields: 12 sliders

INGREDIENTS

¼ pound ham slices

6 large red lettuce leaves

½ cup beer ale cheese (See Page 62)

INSTRUCTIONS

Take a large lettuce leaf and lay it out flat.

Layer a couple slices of ham on leaf.

Spread 1-2 Tablespoons of beer ale cheese on top of the ham.

Starting from the stem end, slowly roll up the leaf.

With a sharp knife gently cut the roll in half, creating two sliders.

Spear each slider with a toothpick to hold it together.

NUTRITION PROFILE

Calories per slider	Total Fat	Total Carb	Sugars	Protein	Sodium	Dietary Fiber
77	3 g	2 g	1 g	11 g	440 mg	0 g

HAM & CHEESE SLIDERS

DEVILED EGGS

Yields: 12 eggs

INGREDIENTS

6 hard boiled eggs (See Best Way to Boil Eggs Page 34)

4 Tablespoons mayonnaise (Page 80)

2 Tablespoons yellow mustard

Pinch of salt

1 teaspoon paprika

2-3 Tablespoons fresh chives, chopped

INSTRUCTIONS

Peel hard boiled eggs and slice in half lengthwise.

Remove the yolks to a small bowl.

Place the whites on a serving platter.

Mash the egg yolks with a fork. Add mayonnaise, mustard, and salt. Mix until it is fully incorporated and creamy.

Spoon about a teaspoon of the yolk mixture into each egg white.

Sprinkle with paprika and chives. Serve cold.

NUTRITION PROFILE

Calories per egg	Total Fat	Total Carb	Sugars	Protein	Sodium	Dietary Fiber
48	3 g	1 g	0 g	3 g	76 mg	0 g

DEVILED EGGS

BEST WAY TO BOIL EGGS

My all-time favorite way to hard boil eggs is to bake them in the oven. It's perfect for when you need to make a big batch at once, in preparation for making deviled eggs or just your weekend snack.

INSTRUCTIONS

Preheat oven to 350° F

Place 1 egg in each slot of a muffin tin

Bake in preheated oven for 30 minutes

Remove the baked eggs and plunge them into a large bowl filled with ice water until completely cooled, 10-15 minutes

"It may be hard for an egg to turn into a bird: it would be a jolly sight harder for it learn to fly while remaining an egg. We are like eggs at present. And you cannot go on indefinitely being just an ordinary, decent egg. We must be hatched or go bad."
– C.S. Lewis

PULLED PORK NACHOS

Serves: 3-4

INGREDIENTS

5 ounces corn tortilla chips
2 cups pulled pork, cooked
1 small onion, chopped
1/3 cup barbecue sauce (See Page 78)
2 ounces cheddar cheese

INSTRUCTIONS

Preheat oven to 350° F.
Spread tortilla chips out on a baking sheet.
Top with pulled pork, onion, barbecue sauce, and cheese.
Bake until cheese is melted (15-20 minutes).
Serve immediately.

 Omit cheddar cheese

NUTRITION PROFILE

Calories per serving	Total Fat	Total Carb	Sugars	Protein	Sodium	Dietary Fiber
249	8 g	30 g	1 g	10 g	244 mg	4 g

BACON WRAPPED POTATOES

Serves: 4-5

INGREDIENTS

4 red potatoes, cut into small pieces (6 pieces per potato)

12 strips of bacon

INSTRUCTIONS

Preheat oven to 350°F.

Prepare a baking sheet by lining it with parchment paper.

Slice each piece of bacon down the middle lengthwise, creating 24 bacon slices.

Roll one bacon slice around each piece of potato and place on baking sheet. Continue until all 24 potato pieces are wrapped.

Bake for 25-30 minutes.

Broil on high for 2-3 minutes for extra crispy bacon.

Transfer potatoes onto a paper towel to drain off.

Serve warm with buffalo dipping sauce (page 76) or ketchup (page 74).

NUTRITION PROFILE

Calories per serving	Total Fat	Total Carb	Sugars	Protein	Sodium	Dietary Fiber
224	7 g	30 g	2 g	10 g	453 mg	3 g

BACON WRAPPED POATOES

Onion Rings – See recipe on Page 46

BAR MUNCHIES

All your favorite bar dishes, without the guilt

BAKED FRENCH FRIES

Serves: 2-3

INGREDIENTS

3 medium russet potatoes

1 ½ Tablespoons olive oil

¼ teaspoon sea salt

INSTRUCTIONS

Preheat oven to 450° F.

Cut potatoes into wedges. (I find using an apple slicer works best.)

Toss potatoes in olive oil and sea salt.

Place on a baking sheet, sprinkle with a little more salt, and bake for 35-40 minutes in the oven.

Serve immediately.

NUTRITION PROFILE

Calories per serving	Total Fat	Total Carb	Sugars	Protein	Sodium	Dietary Fiber
220	7 g	37 g	2 g	4 g	404 mg	4 g

BAKED FRENCH FRIES

FRIED PICKLES
Serves: 3-4

INGREDIENTS

1 cup cornmeal
1/8 teaspoon cayenne pepper
2 teaspoons paprika
2 teaspoons Italian seasoning
3 egg whites
2 Tablespoons half & half or milk
3 cups dill chips
¼ cup potato starch

INSTRUCTIONS

Preheat oven to 350° F.

Prepare a baking sheet by lining it with parchment paper.

On a plate, combine cornmeal, cayenne pepper, paprika, and Italian seasoning.

In a separate bowl, add the egg whites and half & half. Whisk together for 30 seconds.

In a zip top bag, add dill chips and potato starch. Seal bag and shake until pickles are dusted with starch.

Proceed by dipping the chips into the egg mixture, then dredge through the cornmeal mixture.

Arrange the chips evenly across the baking sheet.

Bake for 15 minutes, turn them over, and bake for another 10-15 minutes.

Serve immediately with favorite dipping sauce, ketchup (page 74) or buffalo dip (page 76).

NUTRITION PROFILE

Calories per serving	Total Fat	Total Carb	Sugars	Protein	Sodium	Dietary Fiber
222	2 g	43 g	9 g	6 g	496 mg	2 g

FRIED PICKLES

ONION RINGS

Serves: 3-4

INGREDIENTS

1 cup cornmeal
¼ teaspoon paprika
2 egg whites
2 Tablespoons half & half
2 small onions, cut into ½ inch slices
¼ cup potato starch
Pinch of salt

INSTRUCTIONS

Preheat oven to 450° F.

Prepare a baking sheet by lining it with parchment paper.

In a small bowl, mix cornmeal and stir in paprika

In a separate bowl, combine egg whites and half & half. Whisk together for 30-45 seconds.

In a zip top bag, add the onion slices and potato starch. Seal bag and shake until onions are dusted with starch.

Proceed by dipping an onion slice into the egg mixture, then dredge through cornmeal mixture. Continue until all onion slices are finished.

Place onion slices evenly across the baking sheet. It is ok if they touch a little.

Bake for 12-14 minutes.

Remove from oven and sprinkle with salt.

If desired, serve with homemade ketchup (recipe on page 74).

NUTRITION PROFILE

Calories per serving	Total Fat	Total Carb	Sugars	Protein	Sodium	Dietary Fiber
181	2 g	37 g	.5 g	5 g	40 mg	3 g

ONION RINGS

POTATO WEDGES

Serves: 5-6

INGREDIENTS

5 large red potatoes
2-3 Tablespoons olive oil
1 ½ teaspoons sea salt
2 ounces cheddar cheese
¼ cup green onion, chopped
Optional: Bacon crumbles, sour cream, guacamole (page 64)

INSTRUCTIONS

Preheat oven to 350° F.

Clean red potatoes and pierce a couple times with a knife.

Place in the microwave for 6 minutes, turning them over at 3 minutes. Let potatoes cool for a couple minutes.

Slice potatoes down the middle lengthwise creating two halves. (10 total halves)

Scoop out the center of each piece with a spoon.

Place flat side down on a baking sheet. Brush back sides with olive oil and sprinkle with salt.

Bake for 15-20 minutes.

Take out of the oven and turn the skins over. Brush with olive oil. Add cheese and bacon crumbles, if desired. Bake for 8-10 minutes.

Garnish with green onion and sour cream.

Serve immediately with guacamole (or ketchup, recipe on page 74).

 Omit cheddar cheese
 Omit bacon crumbles

NUTRITION PROFILE

Calories per serving	Total Fat	Total Carb	Sugars	Protein	Sodium	Dietary Fiber
167	8 g	20 g	1 g	5 g	627 mg	2 g

POTATO WEDGES

PICO DE GALLO

Serves: 5-6

INGREDIENTS

5 Roma tomatoes, halved
1 medium white onion
1 jalapeno, seeded
1 teaspoon garlic powder
½ teaspoon chili powder
½ fresh squeezed lime juice

INSTRUCTIONS

In a food processor add all ingredients.

Pulse on low until it reaches desired consistency. (You can make it extra chunky or smooth in texture, depending on your preference.)

Store in the refrigerator up to one week.

Best when served chilled.

NUTRITION PROFILE

Calories per serving	Total Fat	Total Carb	Sugars	Protein	Sodium	Dietary Fiber
34	1 g	7 g	5 g	1 g	12 mg	1 g

BARBECUE BACK RIBS

Serves: 5-6

INGREDIENTS

1 full rack of baby back ribs
1 ½ cups barbecue sauce (Page 78)
¼ cup brown sugar
2 Tablespoons smoked paprika
1 ½ Tablespoons garlic powder
1 ½ Tablespoons onion powder
1 ½ Tablespoons sea salt
1 Tablespoon dry mustard
2 teaspoons cayenne pepper
1 teaspoon black pepper

INSTRUCTIONS

Remove the membrane from ribs before applying the dry rub.

In a small bowl, combine sugar, paprika, garlic powder, onion powder, salt, dry mustard, cayenne pepper, and black pepper.

Mix until fully combined.

Place ribs on a large piece of aluminum foil on baking sheets.

Apply the dry rub evenly on both sides of the ribs. Make sure you get the ends coated, too. Wrap ribs in the foil.

Set in the fridge to marinate. For best results, marinate for 24-48 hours.

Unwrap ribs from foil, coat each side with barbecue sauce, and rewrap back up.

After coating ribs with barbecue sauce, pour a cup of water into crockpot.

Place the foil covered ribs into the crockpot.

For best results, set on low for 8 hours (or on high for 3-4 hours).

Meat will fall right off the bone.

NUTRITION PROFILE

Calories per serving	Total Fat	Total Carb	Sugars	Protein	Sodium	Dietary Fiber
473	34 g	13 g	12 g	28 g	456 mg	1 g

BARBECUE BACK RIBS

CHICKEN FINGERS

Serves: 3-4

INGREDIENTS

1 cup cornmeal

¼ teaspoon paprika

2 egg whites

3 Tablespoons half & half

1 pound thin chicken strips

¼ cup potato starch

INSTRUCTIONS

Preheat oven to 375° F.

Prepare baking sheets by lining with parchment paper.

In a small bowl, mix cornmeal and paprika.

In a separate bowl, combine egg whites and half & half. Whisk together for 30 seconds.

In a zip top bag, add chicken strips and potato starch. Seal bag and shake until chicken strips are dusted with starch.

Proceed by dipping the strips into the egg mixture, then dredge through the cornmeal mixture.

Place strips evenly across the baking sheet.

Bake for 12-15 minutes.

NUTRITION PROFILE

Calories per serving	Total Fat	Total Carb	Sugars	Protein	Sodium	Dietary Fiber
336	4 g	43 g	1 g	40 g	741 mg	2 g

CHICKEN FINGERS

CHEESY GARLIC BREAD

Yields: 8 slices

INGREDIENTS

6 ounces parmesan cheese, shredded

2 ounces white cheddar cheese, shredded

4 ounces cream cheese, softened

2 eggs

2 Tablespoons Italian seasoning

1 Tablespoon butter

1 teaspoon garlic powder

INSTRUCTIONS

Preheat oven to 350° F.

Prepare 9x13 baking sheet by lining with parchment paper.

In a medium bowl, combine 4 ounces of parmesan cheese with white cheddar cheese, cream cheese, eggs, and 1 Tablespoon Italian seasoning.

Stir until fully combined and formed into a cheese-like mixture.

Spoon mixture onto parchment paper and smooth out to edges of pan with a spatula.

Bake for 20-25 minutes. If an air pocket develops (like bread dough sometimes does), just pop it with a knife and let it settle.

Prepare another baking sheet with parchment paper.

Flip the baked cheese bread onto the new baking sheet.

Brush on butter and sprinkle with garlic powder, remaining Italian seasoning, and remaining parmesan cheese.

Return to the oven for another 10 minutes. Remove from oven, slice, and serve immediately.

NUTRITION PROFILE

Calories per serving	Total Fat	Total Carb	Sugars	Protein	Sodium	Dietary Fiber
159	12 g	1 g	.5 g	10 g	367 mg	0 g

CHEESY GARLIC BREAD

BLUE CHEESE SLIDERS

Serves: 5-6

INGREDIENTS

1 pound ground beef

2 ounces blue cheese (approx. ¼ cup, or more for topping)

Pinch of salt and pepper

1 small tomato, sliced

1 green onion, chopped

2-3 leaves of lettuce

INSTRUCTIONS

In a medium bowl, combine ground beef, blue cheese, salt, and pepper. Mix until fully incorporated.

Divide the meat into 20-24 mini-patties.

Gently form each patty into an inch thick disk.

Set frying pan over medium-high heat.

Transfer the burger patties to the hot pan. Cook for 3-4 minutes on one side, then 3-4 minutes on the other side.

Garnish each patty with a slice of tomato, onion, lettuce, and additional blue cheese.

Serve with homemade ketchup (Page 74) if desired.

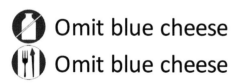

Omit blue cheese

Omit blue cheese

NUTRITION PROFILE

Calories per serving	Total Fat	Total Carb	Sugars	Protein	Sodium	Dietary Fiber
255	20 g	2 g	0 g	17 g	253 mg	0 g

BLUE CHEESE SLIDERS

Queso Dip – See recipe on Page 68

DIPPING, DUNKING, SCOOP WORTHY DIPS

Get your dip on

BEER ALE CHEESE

Yields: 2 cups

INGREDIENTS

2/3 cup gluten-free ale beer
1 1/2 Tablespoons Dijon mustard
1 teaspoon Worcestershire sauce
¼ teaspoon nutmeg
2 ½ ounces cheddar cheese
1 ounce cream cheese
1 Tablespoon potato starch
Pinch of sea salt

INSTRUCTIONS

In a medium saucepan on medium heat, whisk together beer, mustard, Worcestershire sauce, and nutmeg. Whisk frequently to prevent burning.

When beer mixture is warm, add cheddar cheese and cream cheese. Stir until completely melted.

Stir in potato starch a little bit at a time and allow to thicken.

For a thicker dip, add additional potato starch in ¼ teaspoon increments until desired consistency is reached.

Stir in sea salt and serve immediately.

NUTRITION PROFILE

Calories per serving	Total Fat	Total Carb	Sugars	Protein	Sodium	Dietary Fiber
346	22 g	8 g	1 g	13 g	392 mg	0 g

BEER ALE CHEESE

BEST GUACAMOLE EVER

Serves: 2-3

INGREDIENTS

2 ripe avocados, mashed
1 ½ Tablespoons garlic powder
1 Tablespoon onion powder
1 teaspoon cumin powder
½ teaspoon cayenne pepper
2 teaspoons lime juice

INSTRUCTIONS

Place avocados in medium bowl and mash with a fork.
Add garlic, onion, cumin, cayenne, and lime juice.
Mix well until fully combined.
Add more cayenne pepper for more spice, if desired.
Serve chilled with corn tortilla chips.

NUTRITION PROFILE

Calories per serving	Total Fat	Total Carb	Sugars	Protein	Sodium	Dietary Fiber
195	18 g	11 g	1 g	2 g	9 mg	8 g

BEST GUACAMOLE EVER

SPINACH ARTICHOKE DIP

Serves: 4-5

INGREDIENTS

2 teaspoons butter
¼ cup white onion, diced
8 ounces chopped frozen spinach, thawed
4 ounces cream cheese
½ cup sour cream
¼ cup white cheddar cheese

¼ cup parmesan cheese
2 Tablespoons garlic powder
10-12 small artichoke hearts
1 teaspoon lemon juice

INSTRUCTIONS

In a large skillet over medium heat, sauté onion in melted butter until translucent (2-3 minutes).

Add thawed spinach and garlic powder. Cook on medium heat for 5 minutes until warm.

Add cream cheese, sour cream, white cheddar cheese, and parmesan cheese. Turn burner down to low heat and continue stirring until all cheese is melted.

Chop artichoke hearts in half and add to mixture along with lemon juice.

Continue to stir and cook on low heat until dip becomes bubbly and hot (6-8 minutes). Serve immediately.

NUTRITION PROFILE

Calories per serving	Total Fat	Total Carb	Sugars	Protein	Sodium	Dietary Fiber
123	12 g	3 g	0 g	2 g	154 mg	0 g

SPINACH ARTICHOKE DIP

QUESO DIP

Serves: 3-4

INGREDIENTS

6 ounces white cheddar cheese

¼ cup milk

¼ cup pico de gallo or salsa of choice

Pinch of chili powder

INSTRUCTIONS

In a small saucepan, mix cheddar cheese and 2 Tablespoons of milk. Set on low heat.

Stir mixture until cheese begins to evenly melt, then add all but 1-2 Tablespoons of the remaining milk. Mix well, ensuring the mixture will not be too thin before adding the reserved milk.

Add pico de gallo (Page 50) and stir.

Serve hot with corn tortilla chips.

NUTRITION PROFILE

Calories per serving	Total Fat	Total Carb	Sugars	Protein	Sodium	Dietary Fiber
184	14 g	3 g	1 g	12 g	343 mg	0 g

QUESO DIP

HUMMUS DIP

Serves: 5-6

INGREDIENTS

1 (15 ounces) can chickpeas
1/8 cup water
1 Tablespoon minced garlic
2 Tablespoons fresh lemon juice
½ teaspoon cumin
½ teaspoon sea salt
2-3 Tablespoons olive oil
¼ teaspoon paprika

INSTRUCTIONS

Combine all ingredients in a food processor.

Blend on low speed until smooth, scraping sides several times to incorporate everything

If a little dry, add an additional teaspoon of olive oil until it reaches desired consistency.

Sprinkle a little extra paprika over the top before serving.

Serve cold with favorite veggies.

NUTRITION PROFILE

Calories per serving	Total Fat	Total Carb	Sugars	Protein	Sodium	Dietary Fiber
156	7 g	18 g	0 g	4 g	239 mg	4 g

HUMMUS DIP

Barbecue Sauce– See recipe on Page 78

DOLLOP WORTHY CONDIMENTS

HEALTHY KETCHUP

Yields: 2 cups

INGREDIENTS

6 ounces tomato paste

¼ cup honey

1/3 cup apple cider vinegar

1/3 cup + 1 Tablespoon water

1 teaspoon salt

1 teaspoon onion powder

½ teaspoon garlic powder

INSTRUCTIONS

In a small saucepan on low-medium heat, add tomato paste, honey, apple cider vinegar, and 1/3 cup water.

Stir until fully combined.

Stir in salt, onion powder, and garlic powder.

Let simmer 10-15 minutes on low heat.

If mixture is too thick, add additional Tablespoon of water to thin out to desired consistency.

Remove from burner and allow to cool down.

Store in the refrigerator.

NUTRITION PROFILE

Calories per cup	Total Fat	Total Carb	Sugars	Protein	Sodium	Dietary Fiber
198	.5 g	51 g	45 g	4 g	673 mg	4 g

HEALTHY KETCHUP

BUFFALO DIPPING SAUCE

Yields: ½ cup

INGREDIENTS

¼ cup sour cream

2-3 Tablespoons hot sauce of choice

Pinch of paprika

INSTRUCTIONS

In a small bowl, combine all ingredients. If a spicier sauce is desired, add an additional Tablespoon of hot sauce.

Serve cold. Keeps in the refrigerator 1-2 weeks.

NUTRITION PROFILE

Calories per ½ cup	Total Fat	Total Carb	Sugars	Protein	Sodium	Dietary Fiber
123	12 g	3 g	0 g	2 g	154 mg	0 g

BUFFALO DIPPING SAUCE

BARBECUE SAUCE

Yields: 2 cups

INGREDIENTS

2 ½ teaspoons crushed garlic
6 ounces tomato paste
1 Tablespoon onion powder
¼ cup apple cider vinegar
¼ cup Worcestershire sauce
1 Tablespoon chili powder

½ Tablespoon smoked paprika
1 teaspoon liquid smoke
½ Tablespoon salt
¼ cup honey
1 ½ Tablespoons honey mustard

INSTRUCTIONS

In a small saucepan on low-medium heat, add crushed garlic. Let sauté for one minute.

Stir in remaining ingredients until fully combined.

Let simmer 10-15 minutes on low heat.

Remove from burner and allow to cool.

Store in refrigerator. For best flavor, make sauce the day before.

NUTRITION PROFILE

Calories per TBS	Total Fat	Total Carb	Sugars	Protein	Sodium	Dietary Fiber
11	0 g	3 g	2 g	0 g	33 mg	0 g

BARBECUE SAUCE

HOMEMADE MAYONNAISE

Yields: 1 cup

INGREDIENTS

1 large egg yolk, room temperature

2 Tablespoons fresh lemon juice, room temperature

1 Tablespoon honey mustard

½ teaspoon salt

¾ cup light olive oil

INSTRUCTIONS

Combine the room temperature egg yolk, lemon juice, honey mustard, and salt in a small jar. (I prefer a jar rather than a bowl when using an immersion blender.)

Blend together for 10-15 seconds.

With the immersion blender pushed all the way down to the bottom of the jar, continue to blend and begin pouring in the olive oil at a slow, steady stream.

You'll begin to see the magic happen within 2-4 minutes as it starts to turn into a creamy mixture.

Store in the refrigerator in an airtight container up to 2 weeks.

If mixture is not as thick as desired, you can let it sit in the refrigerator and it will thicken slightly OR add about a Tablespoon of potato starch to thicken.

NUTRITION PROFILE

Calories per TBS	Total Fat	Total Carb	Sugars	Protein	Sodium	Dietary Fiber
126	14 g	1 g	0 g	0 g	100 mg	0 g

HOMEMADE MAYONNAISE

METRIC CONVERSIONS

The recipes in this book have not been tested with metric conversions. Some variations may be needed.

General Formula for Metric Conversions

Ounces to grams ounces x 28.35 = grams
Grams to ounces grams x 0.035 = ounces
Pounds to grams pounds x 453.5 = grams
Pounds to kilograms pounds x .45 = kilograms
Cups to liters cups x .24 = liters
Fahrenheit to Celsius (°F -32) x 5 + 9 = °C
Celsius to Fahrenheit (°C x 9) ÷ 5 +32 = °F

Volume/Liquid Measurements

1 teaspoon = 1/6 fluid ounce = 5 milliliters
1 Tablespoon = ½ fluid ounce = 15 milliliters
2 Tablespoons = 1 fluid ounce = 30 milliliters
¼ cup = 2 fluid ounces = 60 milliliters
½ cup = 4 fluid ounces = 118 milliliters
1 cup or ½ pint = 8 fluid ounces = 250 milliliters
2 cups or 1 pint = 16 fluid ounces = 500 milliliters
4 cups or 1 quart = 32 fluid ounces = 1,000 milliliters
1 gallon = 4 liters

INDEX

A
Artichokes
  Spinach Artichoke Dip, 66
Avocado
  Best Guacamole Ever, 64

B
Bacon
  Bacon Wrapped Potatoes, 38
  Jalapeño Poppers, 22
Barbecue Sauce, 78
Beans
  Cheesy Chili Cheese Dip, 26

C
Cheese
  Cheesy Chili Cheese Dip, 26
  Queso Dip, 68
  Spinach Artichoke Dip, 66
  Cheesy Garlic Bread, 56
  Beer Ale Cheese, 62
Chicken
  Chicken Fingers, 54
  Buffalo Chicken Meatballs, 28
Chickpeas
  Hummus Dip, 70

Condiments
  Homemade Mayonnaise, 80
  Barbecue Sauce, 78
  Healthy Ketchup, 74
Cornmeal
  Fried Pickles, 44
  Onion Rings, 46
  Chicken Fingers, 54
Cream Cheese
  Spinach Artichoke Dip, 66

D
Deviled Eggs, 32
Dips
  Cheesy Chili Cheese Dip, 26
  Hummus Dip, 70
  Queso Dip, 68
  Pico De Gallo, 50
  Spinach Artichoke Dip, 66
  Best Guacamole Ever, 64

E

Eggs
  Deviled Eggs, 32
  Best Way to Boil Eggs, 34
  Homemade Mayonnaise, 80

F

Fried Pickles, 44
French Fries, 42

G

Garlic
  Spinach Artichoke Dip, 66
  Cheesy Garlic Bread, 56

Green Onion
  Loaded Potato Nachos, 24
  Cheesy Chili Cheese Dip, 26
  Potato Wedges, 48
  Blue Cheese Sliders, 58

H

Half & Half
  Cheesy Chili Cheese Dip, 26
  Fried Pickles, 44
  Onion Rings, 46
  Chicken Fingers, 54

Ham
  Ham & Cheese Sliders, 30

Hummus Dip, 70

J

Jalapeño
  Jalapeño Poppers, 22
  Pico De Gallo, 50

K

L

Lettuce
  Blue Cheese Sliders, 58
  Ham & Cheese Sliders, 30

Lime
  Pico De Gallo, 50
  Best Guacamole Ever, 64

M

Homemade Mayonnaise, 80

Mustard
  Deviled Eggs, 32
  Barbecue Back Ribs, 52
  Beer Ale Cheese, 62

N

Nutmeg
  Beer Ale Cheese, 62

O

Olive Oil
  Baked French Fries, 42

Onion
  Pulled Pork Nachos, 36
  Onion Rings, 46
  Pico De Gallo, 50

Onion Powder
  Buffalo Chicken Meatballs, 28
  Barbecue Back Ribs, 52
  Best Guacamole Ever, 64
  Healthy Ketchup, 74

P

Paprika
  Deviled Eggs, 32
Parmesan
  Cheesy Garlic Bread, 56
  Spinach Artichoke Dip, 66
Pico De Gallo, 50
Potato
  Loaded Potato Nachos, 24
  Bacon Wrapped Potatoes, 38
  Baked French Fries, 42
  Potato Wedges, 48
Potato Starch
  Cheesy Chili Cheese Dip, 26
  Buffalo Chicken Meatballs, 28
  Beer Ale Cheese, 62

Q

Queso Dip, 68

R

Russet Potatoes
  Baked French Fries, 42

S

Sour Cream
  Spinach Artichoke Dip, 66
  Buffalo Dipping Sauce, 76
Sugar
  Barbecue Back Ribs, 52

T

Tomato
  Pico De Gallo, 50
  Blue Cheese Sliders, 58

Tomato Paste
  Healthy Ketchup, 74
  Barbecue Sauce, 78

U

V

Vegan
  Baked French Fries, 42
  Pico De Gallo, 50
  Best Guacamole Ever, 64
  Hummus Dip, 70
  Healthy Ketchup, 74
  Barbecue Sauce, 78
Vegetarian
  Deviled Eggs, 32
  Baked French Fries, 42
  Fried Pickles, 44
  Onion Rings, 46
  Pico De Gallo, 50
  Cheesy Garlic Bread, 56
  Beer Ale Cheese, 62
  Spinach Artichoke Dip, 66
  Queso Dip, 68
  Hummus Dip, 70
  Healthy Ketchup, 74
  Buffalo Dipping Sauce, 76
  Barbecue Sauce, 78
  Homemade Mayonnaise, 80

W

White Cheddar Cheese
  Queso Dip, 68

X

Y

Z

About the Author

Lindsay Garza is the personality behind the Veggie Balance blog. She lives with her husband in DeWitt, Michigan with their dog and two cats. Favorite things include her camera, running, warm tea, and super dark chocolate.

Made in the USA
Charleston, SC
14 November 2015